Did

P

A MISCELLANY

GW00507191

Compiled by Julia Skinner

With particular reference to the work of John Bainbridge,
Roger Crisp, Roger Guttridge, Leigh Hatts and Marion Marples

THE FRANCIS FRITH COLLECTION

Christmas
Hazel
25.12.14

www.francisfrith.com

First published in the United Kingdom in 2012 by The Francis Frith Collection®

This edition published exclusively for Bradwell Books in 2012
For trade enquiries see: www.bradwellbooks.com or tel: 0800 834 920
ISBN 978-1-84589-689-8

British Library Cataloguing in Publication Data

Did You Know? Poole - A Miscellany
Compiled by Julia Skinner
With particular reference to the work of John Bainbridge, Roger Crisp, Roger Guttridge,
Leigh Hatts and Marion Marples

The Francis Frith Collection
Oakley Business Park,
Wylye Road, Dinton,
Wiltshire SP3 5EU
Tel: +44 (0) 1722 716 376
Email: info@francisfrith.co.uk
www.francisfrith.com

Printed and bound in Malaysia
Contains material sourced from responsibly managed forests

Front Cover: **POOLE, HIGH STREET 1904** 52808p
Frontispiece: **POOLE, THE QUAY 1931** 84909

The colour-tinting is for illustrative purposes only, and is not intended to be historically accurate

CONTENTS

INTRODUCTION

Poole developed as a port and mercantile centre along the banks of the finest natural harbour in England; the earliest area of settlement is the part now known as the Old Town, which grew up around the older quays. Poole is now one of the largest towns along the south coast but still maintains strong links with the sea, having become a mecca for yachtsmen and other sailors as well as remaining a working port. Nowadays the Borough of Poole is made up of numerous suburbs and neighbourhoods spreading out from the old, historic town, many of which developed from villages that were absorbed into Poole as the town grew. The borough is a unitary authority with a modern boundary, but it neatly brings back within one council the land between the River Stour and the coast which was the original estate of Canford manor, near Wimborne, out of which Poole was born.

There was much unemployment and poverty in Poole in the mid 20th century, but the decades following the Second World War were a time of extraordinary industrial growth in the town, which attracted a number of major national companies seeking to relocate after the war. This triggered a major house-building spree, and more than 10,000 new homes were built in Poole between 1946 and 1966. Of these, around 4,000 were council houses and flats, the vast majority on the new Bourne, Trinidad, Alderney and Turlin Moor estates, or in the Old Town, where several tower blocks appeared. Running parallel to this was a slum clearance programme – many houses in the ancient, narrow streets and alleys of the Old Town were damp, rodent-infested slums, and in the late 1950s and early 1960s almost 1,000 condemned houses were demolished, and their occupants re-homed by the council. Unfortunately many historic buildings were also demolished at this time, particularly in the Old Town, but a Conservation Area was created in the town centre in 1975 to

preserve what was left of Poole's most notable buildings, and there is still much fine Georgian and Victorian architecture to be seen.

By the 1960s Poole's population had grown to around 100,000 inhabitants, yet the demand for new homes was still not satisfied, and another growth phase began. A show house that was formally opened at Canford Heath in November 1963 was the first of thousands to be built on the heathland north of Poole, much of which had been used for military exercises during the war – it had to be cleared of unexploded shells before development could begin. The Canford Heath developments heralded a decade in which Poole became the fastest-growing town in the UK, apart from designated 'new towns'. Smaller developments followed at Hamworthy, Merley, Broadstone and Creekmoor, all of which are now included in the Borough of Poole. These developments took Poole's population to 138,000 by the millennium.

The Quay is still the historic heart that drives the town. The days are long gone when pirate ships used to lurk off Studland to waylay the shipping using Poole's busy harbour, as are the Newfoundland cod ships that brought huge wealth to the town in its Golden Age of the 18th century, but the modern, colourful Quay remains a busy, bustling place, especially in summer when vessels of various kinds and sizes can be seen moored three or four abreast, and occasionally an elegant tall ship or a celebrity's luxury yacht will put into port. Across the water at Hamworthy the cargo vessels, the timber stacked high in Sydenhams' Quayside yards, the newly- or partly-built Sunseeker yachts and the cross-Channel ferries which daily ply between Hamworthy and France are a reminder that Poole is still a working port and not just a tourist attraction; so too are the rows of trawlers and small fishing boats opposite the Lifeboat Museum east of the Quay. Poole is a town with its feet firmly in the past whilst it looks forward to a bright future, but its life will always revolve around the harbour and Quay, and its gaze will always be looking out to sea.

DORSET DIALECT
WORDS AND PHRASES

'Bibber' - to shiver with cold.

'Blather' - an uproar, a noise, a fuss.

'Chippols' - young onions.

'Culver' - a wood pigeon.

'Limber' - slender.

'Maggotty' - fanciful.

'Tinklebobs' - icicles.

'Quilkin' - a frog.

'Thic' - that.

'Gurt' - great, large.

'Cassn't' - can't.

'Mommet' - a cute, sweet or good child.

'Wagwant' - a whining or naughty child.

'Thunder-daisies' - ox-eye daisies

'Dumbledore' - a bumblebee.

'Yaffle' - a green woodpecker.

HAUNTED POOLE

A number of pubs in the Old Town of Poole are reputed to be haunted. The Crown Hotel in Market Street is perhaps the most famous. The story goes that in the 17th century a landlord of the inn had two deformed twin children. He kept them out of sight, imprisoned in an upstairs room of the hotel's stable block, before eventually killing them – and, indeed, a hidden attic room with no door was discovered in 1966 when the old stable block was converted into a night-club venue. It is said that the sound of crying children can be heard in that part of the inn by those with ears to listen. Other spooky phenomena reported in the hotel include a strange moving ball of light on the stairs and the sound of a piano playing in an empty room. The King Charles Inn in Thames Street is reputed to be haunted by the unhappy shade of the 'hanged lady' whose sailor lover was lost at sea; in despair she hanged herself from the beams of an upper room in the building. A happier spirit said to roam the hostelry is a ghostly laughing fisherman, and the mysterious apparition of a little girl has also been reported there. The sound of unearthly dogs barking has been heard at the Blue Boar in Market Close, where some people have also been aware of the strong, unexplained scents of lavender and tobacco. Staff working there have reported seeing strange misty figures around the pub which either suddenly disappeared or glided away through the walls of the building.

Away from pubs, the historic medieval house in the lower High Street known as Scaplen's Court (see page 19) was once the home of a rich widow called Alice Green and her maid Agnes Beard, who were brutally murdered there in 1598. The apron-wearing ghost of Agnes Beard reputedly haunts the building, but she is not alone; other ghostly figures roaming Scaplen's Court include a bearded man wearing a long cloak, and another man from a more recent era, who wears a bowler hat – an image of this restless spirit was captured on CCTV in 2008, in the first-floor Solar Room of the building…

POOLE MISCELLANY

In 1964 a dredger working in Poole Harbour brought to light a long wooden object found preserved in a layer of peat in Brownsea Roads, which turned out to be part of an Iron Age canoe that had been hewed out of a huge oak trunk. A diver later recovered a second section. Put together, the two pieces indicate that the vessel measured 10 metres (33 feet) from stern to prow, 1.22 metres (4 feet) at its widest point, with a draught of about 30cms (12 inches). It has been estimated that the boat could carry around 18 people. Radio-carbon dating has dated the Poole logboat to around 295BC, making it about 2,300 years old. Its shallow draught made it ideally suited to a harbour which even now only has an average depth of 48cms (1.57 feet), with one main dredged channel through the harbour from the mouth to Holes Bay. The logboat can be seen in Poole Museum at the lower end of the High Street in the Old Town area.

POOLE, AN IRON AGE LOGBOAT IN POOLE MUSEUM 2004 P72701

In 2002 archaeologists made a discovery which led to Poole being described as Britain's oldest-known cross-Channel port. The remains of two jetties extending from Green Island and Cleavel Point on the south side of the harbour provide evidence that there was a flourishing port here 200 years before the Roman invasion of Britain in AD43. Timber pilings excavated from a deep layer of silt on the sea bed were radio-carbon dated at 250BC, making these the oldest substantial port structures so far discovered anywhere on the British coast. The remains suggest this was an Iron Age trading complex, with the massive stone and timber jetties reaching out into the deep water channel providing berths for large ocean-going ships – raising the possibility that perhaps Greek and Roman traders made the journey from the Mediterranean to the Dorset coast. Two jetties have been traced, one with a length of 80 metres (263 feet) and the other with a surviving length of 45 metres (150 feet) but probably originally the same. The jetties were built up from tons of rock and rubble, reinforced with hundreds of oak tree trunks, sharpened at one end so they could be rammed into the sea bed, then surfaced with a smooth paving of shaped flagstones. The scale of the huge construction work implies they were made by a large, skilled and organised workforce.

The vast expanse of Poole Harbour is the largest natural harbour in Europe and one of several contenders for the title of the second largest in the world after Sydney Harbour in Australia, comprising 100 miles of sheltered coastline and 10,000 acres of tidal water. However, it was not a harbour at all until about 6,000BC, when rising seas following the end of the last Ice Age broke through a chalk ridge that ran between the chalk stacks known as Old Harry Rocks, on the coast of the Isle of Purbeck east of Studland, and the Needles, off the Isle of Wight. Before then, the 'harbour' was a river valley which ran eastwards from Poole and along what is now the Solent to enter the sea beyond Southampton and the Isle of Wight.

The Roman Conquest of Britain began in AD43, and the Romans used Poole Harbour as an invasion port during their conquest of south-west England. The Roman general who led the campaign in this part of the country was Vespasian, who went on to become the Roman Emperor. The Romans built their landing facilities at Hamworthy (the exact site is as yet unknown), from where they constructed a road to their 40-acre base camp at Lake Gates, between Corfe Mullen and Wimborne. From there, other Roman roads led off to the north, west and east.

Two local industries which were already flourishing on the harbour shores at the time of the Roman Conquest of Britain in the first century AD were salt-making and pottery. Several Iron Age salt-making sites have been discovered. The technique used was to boil seawater in pottery containers until only the salt remained. Salt-making continued in the Poole area for many centuries, as evidenced in the original name of The Salterns for the area now called Lilliput, which was in active use for salt-making from the 1730s, if not earlier. Poole Library holds a map dated 1748 which shows the lagoon, together with the area that is now Salterns Way and Lilliput shops, as 'salt works belonging to Sir Thomas Webb baronet' (Sir Thomas was the local Lord of the Manor at that time), with two Boiling Houses near the edge of the harbour. The use of the lagoon as salt pans, and of the surrounding areas for the salt manufacturing processes, continued well into the 19th century, but by the time of an Admiralty survey in 1849 the lagoon is noted as 'Old Salterns', by which date salt-making there had ceased. Today, the area's salt-making heritage is recalled in the names of the Salterns Harbourside Hotel, Salterns Marina and Salterns Way in Lilliput and Salterns Road in Lower Parkstone.

POOLE, THE QUAY 1908 61172

The extensive clay deposits around Poole Harbour have made Poole a pottery-producing area throughout its recorded history; this led to the establishment of a number of important pottery businesses in the area in the 19th century, the most famous of which became the renowned Poole Pottery (see page 35). The Romans made good use of the Poole Harbour potters, whose black burnished ware was distributed to the whole of Roman Britain. Their pots have been found as far north in England as Hadrian's Wall. This view of Poole Quay, taken from Poole Bridge, shows a barge typical of those which, until the 1950s, brought clay from the nearby Purbeck peninsula for use in Poole's local potteries as well as for export overseas. The tall ships seen in the background on the right are moored at Ballast Quay, so-named after the ballast which was loaded into ships there prior to sailing.

The name of the settlement of Poole is very ancient, since the Celtic word 'pwll' and the Old English word 'pool' both mean 'a large expanse of water', or 'a place by a pool, or creek'. The name originally referred to the inner harbour now called Holes Bay – 'the Pool'. The earliest part of Poole developed on the small peninsula now known as the 'Old Town' and Quay – the discovery of Saxon pottery in Thames Street and at Baiter Green suggests some occupation of the area at this period, but it was probably just a small fishing village. Poole was not even mentioned in the Domesday Book of 1086, although the area's parent manor of Canford, near Wimborne, is included.

In Saxon and early Norman times, it was Wareham rather than Poole that served as the main port for east Dorset. There are several reasons for the decline of Wareham and the rise of Poole as east Dorset's main port in the late 12th and 13th centuries, but a major factor was probably the ambitions of the local Lords of the Manor of Canford to develop a seaport of their own. The fledgling town with its seaport was well established by 1224, for in that year 'La Pole' appears in a list of the 24 principal ports of the kingdom.

In 1239 a charter was granted to the Lord of the Manor, William Longspée, which allowed him the right to hold a weekly market at Poole on Tuesdays and an annual market on St Margaret's Day (20 July) and the two following days. However, nine years later, in 1248, Longspée decided to sell much of his controlling interest in the port to raise finance so he could take part in a crusade to the Holy Land. For the price of 70 marks, Poole's merchants and ship-owners were able to buy, among other things, 'all kinds of liberties' concerning themselves and their goods, including exemption from most of the tolls due to Longspée. The charter allowed the maritime community at La Pole to set up a town council, with the right to appoint six burgesses to govern their town, and hold a local court. The Longspée Charter survives to this day in the Poole archives.

Poole was granted further rights under the Montacute Charter of 1371, signed by the Lord of Canford Manor, William Montacute, Earl of Salisbury, including permission to call its first citizen 'mayor' rather than port-reeve. In status terms, Poole took a significant step forward in 1568, when Queen Elizabeth I granted a charter which greatly increased the town's independence by giving it corporate county status. This Great Charter gave Poole the right to hold land and property, to elect its own Sheriff or monarch's representative, to hold regular courts including Quarter Sessions, and to keep any fines imposed instead of handing them over to the Lord of the Manor at Canford. The two most important charters in Poole's history, the Longspée Charter and the Great Charter, are represented by the two supporters depicted on the coat of arms of Poole Borough Council: to the left is a gold lion holding a long sword, representing the crusading knight William Longspée; on the right is a dragon derived from the Royal Arms of Elizabeth I.

POOLE, HIGH STREET 1900 46087

POOLE, THE TOWN CELLARS 1887 19511

In 1433 Poole was made Dorset's Port of the Staple, licensed to handle the import and export of staple commodities – mainly wool, woolfells (skins of sheep with the fleece still attached) and leather. Export duties on wool soon accounted for 80% of the local customs revenue. The stone building known as the Town Cellars at the junction of Thames Street with the Quay dates from this time; it was built to house the 'commodities of the staple' awaiting export and is called the Woolhouse in some medieval documents. It is one of the finest surviving examples of a woolhouse in England and was the largest in northern Europe when first built – it was originally much longer than it is now, but was cut in two in the 1780s when Thames Street was driven through it to join up with the Quay. The longer section of the building now houses the Local History Centre and contains a magnificent timber-beamed roof, while across Thames Street a shorter section survives as part of the King Charles pub (the building with the open upper storey door behind the Harbour Office in the photograph on the opposite page).

Sarum Street is a small lane off Thames Street, in front of the King Charles pub, which runs behind the Town Cellars building. There is a low, stone outbuilding built against the back of the Town Cellars with the date 1820 inscribed in the lintel stone above the doorway. The iron bars in the two windows are the clue to its former use as gaol. It also has an iron ceiling to prevent escapes.

Photograph 52815 (below) shows the handsome building at the junction of Thames Street and the Quay that is now used by the Coastguard service, but when this photograph was taken it was the Harbour Office. It was originally built to provide a club and reading room for ships' captains and town merchants. The building dates from 1727; the first floor was extended over the pavement in 1822 to allow for a fire and chimney in the Ballast Master's office above. On the front of the building is a sundial dedicated to S Weston, Mayor of Poole in 1814, and on the side wall is a relief carving of a bewigged Benjamin Skutt who was Mayor of Poole three times, in 1717, 1727 and 1742.

POOLE, THE HARBOUR OFFICE 1904 52815

POOLE, ST JAMES'S CHURCH 1908 61161

Thames Street leads up from the Quay to St James's Church. The church was rebuilt between 1819 and 1820 but some features from the earlier structure were retained. These include the organ, which dates from 1799, and the mahogany reredos which was given to the church in 1736; painted in gold lettering on its panels are the words of the Lord's Prayer, the Ten Commandments, and the Creed. The roof is supported by ten quatrefoil columns fashioned from the trunks of pine trees from Newfoundland; they were brought over on the decks of Poole sailing brigs and reflect the town's historical trading links with Newfoundland, particularly with cod fishery. Some years ago a Poole vicar sent a message to his opposite number in the Newfoundland port of Twillingate inviting him to return the gas-lamps 'loaned' to the church there 150 years earlier. Twillingate's quick-witted priest replied that he would be happy to do so if Poole returned the pillars supporting St James's roof! In the 1908 photograph on the opposite page they are painted to resemble stone, but they have now been stripped back to their natural wood.

Nowadays, the interior of St James's Church is festooned with colourful flags and shields, including the shield (or coat of arms) of Poole, which features a dolphin, representing the importance of the fishing industry to Poole; St James's Church has the Poole dolphin on its weathervane, and is sometimes called 'the fishermen's church'. There is also a fishing theme in a lovely modern stained glass memorial window by John Callan at the back of the church; in graduations of rich blues and yellows, it shows a fishing net full of fish in the sea, most of which are swimming towards the sunlight flickering on the surface of the water. Poole's coat of arms also features three scallop shells. These recall the pilgrimage many people made in the Middle Ages to the shrine of St James in Santiago de Compostela in Galicia, a region of north-west Spain. The scallop shell was the symbol of the Santiago pilgrim, and Poole adopted the shells on its coat of arms because so many people used to embark from here when making this journey.

POOLE, ST JAMES'S CHURCH, THE INTERIOR 1908 61160

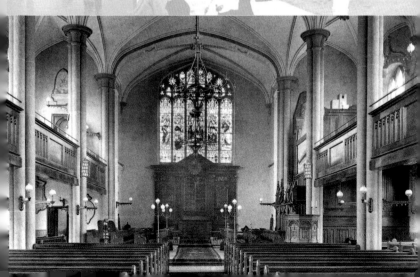

One of the local seafarers in the 15th century who took pilgrims from Poole to the ports of the Galician coast was probably the most notorious character in the town's history – the sea captain and pirate Harry Pay, who was licensed in 1401 to take up to 80 pilgrims to Spain in his ship the 'Mary'. Unfortunately, he also sometimes sailed across the Bay of Biscay to raid the Spanish coast. To avoid detection Pay sometimes flew a French flag. In the early 15th century he became a thorn in the side of the French and Spanish, who knew him as 'Arripay'; one Spanish chronicler described him as a 'knight who scours the sea as a corsair with many ships, plundering all the Spanish and French vessels he can encounter'. Of those recorded, Pay's most successful expedition was in 1407 when he brought home no less than 120 vessels captured off the Brittany coast, laden with iron, salt and oil.

However, Harry Pay's actions had grave consequences for his home town. Angered by his attacks on their shipping, in 1405 the French and Spanish joined forces and sent a small army of crossbowmen into the harbour in five galleys and two smaller ships to attack Poole as a reprisal raid, burning and looting much of the medieval town in revenge for Pay's deeds. The dawn attack took the people of Poole by surprise and it was some time before they were able to organise their archers and men-at-arms, but they put up a stern defence as battle raged in the alleys linking the Quay with the High Street, removing the doors of their houses to use as shields against the enemy's crossbow bolts. Much damage was done to the town and there were many casualties. Harry Pay himself was away at sea at the time, and missed it all. His home was among the few houses to escape destruction, but his brother was among those killed.

The Franco-Spanish attack on Poole of 1405 caused great devastation, and it was many years before Poole recovered its importance as a major port and trading centre. By 1542, however, when King Henry VIII's travelling topographer John Leland visited the town, it was back on the road to growth and prosperity. 'Within living memory, much good building has taken place, and trade has greatly increased', Leland noted, adding that the town was entered via a 'fortified stone gate'. Part of the deal when Poole was made a Port of the Staple in 1433 was that the citizens had to 'wall, embattle and fortify the town' to protect both local and visiting merchants. The defences they constructed included a 'town ditch' dug across the narrow neck of land joining the Poole peninsular to the mainland, which roughly corresponded to the route of the present railway line. Behind this ditch they built defensive walls, through which the only entrance into the town was over a drawbridge and through the town gate – a stone gatehouse flanked by two towers. For some reason the gate was built not in the High Street but a hundred yards or so to the west, accessed by Towngate Lane which branched off the High Street to lead to it. The old town gate was demolished in the late 17th century, but Towngate Lane still remained the main route out of town.

During the Civil War of the 17th century, Poole's puritan stance and its merchants' opposition to the ship money tax imposed by King Charles I led to the town declaring for Parliament, unlike its Royalist neighbours Wimborne and Corfe Castle. In fact it was the 600-strong Parliamentary garrison from Poole that besieged Corfe Castle on the Purbeck peninsula in 1643 and was famously resisted by Lady Bankes and a few servants. Poole in turn resisted a Royalist attempt to seize it in September 1643, when Captain Francis Sydenham was bribed to open the town gate to the king's forces during his stint on watch. Sydenham went along with the deal, but promptly informed the town governor, who organised his soldiers to ambush the invaders as they tried to enter the town.

POOLE, CHURCH STREET, ALMSHOUSES 1908 61170

This photograph shows the distinctive stone St George's Almshouses in Church Street, one of the oldest parts of Poole. The almshouses were first built in the 1400s by the Fraternity (or Guild) of St George, a forerunner of the friendly society, but have been much altered over the years. The building was originally a single hall, possibly divided by partitions, but upper rooms were added in the 17th century. Further alterations were carried out in 1904 and again in 1970, when the building was renovated and its accommodation for old people modernised. This photograph was taken in 1908 after they had been restored in 1904 to provide accommodation for five retired people, as commemorated with a tablet on the wall over the doors of the building: 'This tablet was erected AD 1904. These almshouses first built in the reign of Henry V and long the property of St George's Guild passed to the Crown in 1547 and were purchased for the Corporation in 1550. They have been devoted to the use of the poor for over 500 years.' They are still lived in.

One of Poole's oldest buildings is next to the King's Head pub in the lower High Street, yet it took a violent gale in 1923 to unveil its medieval features. The storm caused a chimney stack to collapse, and the damage this caused revealed medieval features behind later layers of brick, wood and plaster. The Chief Inspector of Ancient Monuments described it as 'one of the finest examples of a 15th-century town house on the south coast'. The building is now Scaplen's Court Museum and is used as an educational centre for school children, but its herb garden is open to the public in summer. The King's Head pub next to Scalpen's Court is one of the oldest pubs in Poole although it has been much rebuilt and renovated over the centuries. It was previously called the Plume of Feathers, but its present name commemorates King Henry VIII (1491-1547), who reputedly stayed there in the 16th century when he came to view the building of a castle on Brownsea Island in Poole Harbour.

POOLE, SCAPLEN'S COURT 2004 P72708

The long shoreline and many inlets of Poole Harbour and the beaches and chines around Poole Bay outside the harbour made this an ideal area in the past for smugglers to land their cargoes of contraband goods, mostly brandy, gin, rum, wine, tea and tobacco, all of which were heavily taxed. However, for some smugglers it was easier just to pay the corrupt Poole Quay officials to turn a blind eye to an illegal cargo being landed – in the late 17th century they were notorious for their willingness to be bribed, and in 1678 the Customs Collector for Poole was dismissed for fraud whilst collaborating with smugglers. Many prominent people in the town were also involved in smuggling, and a report into corruption in the ports in 1682 identified two of Poole's leading citizens as smugglers: past and present mayors Moses Durrell, a pioneer non-conformist, and John Carter, a local merchant and magistrate, who ran the Carter Gang, one of the most infamous of the local smuggling gangs. They hid their contraband all over town, and even built a special landing stage at Baiter to bring in their smuggled goods. Because John Carter was also in business in the town as a legitimate merchant, this allowed him to run a number of covers for his illegal operations and gave him access to all sorts of stores and hiding places for his contraband goods – his businesses included a windmill, a malthouse and brewery, a shop, various stables, cellars, barley lofts and wood yards, all of which were used for hiding contraband. Members of the Carter Gang disguised themselves by wearing masks and tall women's hats, carried swords and heavy clubs to intimidate any opposition to their activities, and generally terrorized the local inhabitants.

Nor did matters improve much in the 18th century, when Poole's unsavoury reputation for bribery, corruption and evil-doing gave rise to a saying in the surrounding area that:

> *'If Poole was a fish-pool, and the men of Poole fish,*
> *There'd be a pool for the devil, and fish for his dish.'*

**POOLE
SHIPS AT THE QUAY
c1880** P72501

One of the iconic buildings of Poole is the old Custom House on the Quay, now a wine bar and restaurant (photograph 52814, opposite). This Custom House dates from 1813, but in 1747 its predecessor was the scene of the most famous smuggling incident in British history, when thirty smugglers (including members of the notorious Hawkhurst Gang) rode to Poole from Kent and Sussex to 'rescue' a cargo of tea that had been seized by revenue men from their cutter the 'Three Brothers' near Christchurch. They tied up the town's night-watchman, broke into the Custom House and then rode off in triumph with their cargo. The incident had a tragic sequel when a witness and a Customs officer were intercepted by members of the gang while on their way to give evidence against them, and were brutally murdered. The smugglers were eventually rounded up and tried for the break-in, the two murders and other crimes, and a number of them were hanged.

No local smuggler was more successful than Isaac Gulliver (1746-1822), who ran a huge smuggling operation that extended across Dorset and into Devon, Wiltshire and Hampshire; his men even wore a uniform. He made a fortune from smuggling, but proudly claimed never to have killed a man in the course of his career. He lived for much of his life at Kinson, a few miles from Poole, which was then a village in the Manor of Canford, but now part of north Bournemouth. In his house he had a secret room that was entered from a door ten feet up the chimney, and beneath the house were underground tunnels which led in all directions – legend says that one went as far as Parkstone! Local residents have long wondered whether there was a connection between Isaac Gulliver and the name of the Poole district of Lilliput, given the literary connection of the two names in Jonathan Swift's popular novel 'Gulliver's Travels', first published in 1726. It is distinctly possible, since Isaac Gulliver did own property in the area (including Flag Farm, and possibly Lilliput House); the district was previously called The Saltings and no other explanation has been offered for its new name, which may be an example of 18th-century humour.

The structure seen in front of the Custom House in this photograph (behind the two boys) is still there today. It is the large cross beam, or Town Beam, which was used for weighing goods in order to work out the customs duty payable. There is now an informative metal plaque at its crosspoint, pointing out the metal eyelets at the end of each wooden arm used in the weighing procedure, and through which ran the 'steelyards'.

**POOLE
THE CUSTOM HOUSE
1904** 52814

23

POOLE

A MISCELLANY

Another of Poole's iconic buildings is the Guildhall in Market Street, also known as the Town Hall and the Market House; with its elegant fan of twin staircases, it looks very similar to the old Custom House. Its white central dome is topped with a weathervane of a Poole dolphin. The Guildhall was built in 1761 with provision for a market on the ground floor, with open-fronted stalls selling all the variety of wares to be expected in such a busy port with trading links as far afield as Newfoundland and the Mediterranean. On the upper floor were the Corporation Meeting Room and the Courtroom, and Poole Council continued to meet there until 1931. The Guildhall's backdrop has changed somewhat since this photograph was taken in 1904. The buildings to the immediate left of this photograph are still there, including the Angel Inn (the building with a chimney in its dormer), but the Police Station behind the Guildhall to the right was destroyed by fire in the Second World War.

POOLE, THE GUILDHALL 1904 52812

As well as market scenes around the Guildhall in the past, there were the comings and goings of political hustings, proclamations, and the announcing of sentences from the court which could lead onto the spectacle of public floggings or deportations to America, or both.

The Guildhall has played various roles in the more recent history of the town. During the Second World War of the 20th century it was used as a canteen and meeting room for American soldiers who were stationed in the area prior to the invasion of France in the D-Day landings of 1944. Showers and washing facilities for the servicemen were installed in the Guildhall at this time, which were later converted into public baths for the townspeople that remained in use until the 1960s. The building served as Poole's museum from 1971 until 1991, but then stood empty and unused for the next 16 years, until it was the subject of a renovation project funded by Poole Borough Council. The restored Guildhall was re-opened in 2007, and this beautiful building now serves the town as a Register Office, where weddings, civil partnerships and other civic ceremonies take place.

After local government was reformed under the Municipal Corporations Act of 1835, the town clerk Robert Parr lost his job; as a result he put in an inflated compensation claim. Many householders refused to pay the resultant rate rise, and this in turn pushed the town corporation to the point of insolvency. In 1839 bailiffs seized the corporation's assets, including the Guildhall itself, and its furniture, maces and ancient seals, and the High Court handed them to Mr Parr, who leased the Guildhall to a farmer. So serious was the financial crisis for the town that the council had no money to help the poor, feed the prisoners in the town jail or even buy the gas for the street lights – the formation of the Poole Gas Company in 1833 had made Poole one of the first towns in the south of England to have illuminated streets.

**POOLE, HIGH STREET, BEECH HURST
1904** 52809

Poole's prosperity for many centuries was due to its involvement in the Newfoundland cod trade. By the 18th century hundreds of ships were sailing from Poole for the Grand Banks off Newfoundland each spring and returning with cargoes of salt-dried cod, as well as furs, sealskins and cranberries. They also took their salt-cod to the Mediterranean countries and West Indies to sell, then brought exotic cargos like almonds, figs, lemons, wine and oil back to Poole. The Poole merchants who ran the trade grew very rich and many of the Georgian mansions they built with their profits still stand in the town, such as Poole House and the Mansion House in Thames Street, Jolliffe House in West Street and Beech Hurst in the High Street, which was built in the 1790s by Samuel Rolles, who had his family crest placed above its entrance. The Mansion House in Thames Street, now a hotel, was built in the 1770s by the brothers Isaac and Benjamin Lester, who ran the biggest fleet in the cod trade. They celebrated the object of their success in their home with two fillets of dried codfish carved in marble decorating the fireplace of what is now the Lester-Garland room in the hotel (photograph P72705, opposite).

POOLE, MANSION HOUSE, MARBLE COD FILLETS ABOVE THE FIREPLACE, LESTER-GARLAND ROOM 2004 P72705

Thousands of people were employed servicing the Newfoundland trade, in both Poole and Newfoundland – more than a third of today's Newfoundlanders are descended from ancestors who originally sailed from Poole. Some of those sailors or workers in the cod trade chose to settle on Newfoundland, but others were forced to stay there after Poole's cod trade crashed to a dramatic halt following the end of the Napoleonic Wars in 1815, leaving them unemployed and so impoverished they could not afford the passage home. After years of near-monopoly of the trade, Poole's merchants now found themselves competing with fleets from America, France and Norway. The price of salt-cod fell dramatically, and many Poole merchants went bankrupt. By 1828 there were only 10 British ships fishing in Newfoundland waters.

Reminders of the town's historic connection with Newfoundland can be found in some of modern Poole's street names, such as Newfoundland Drive, Labrador Drive and Cabot Way, and the link is also commemorated with a map of Newfoundland on the ankle-high tile frieze at the Barber's Wharf residential development on the Quay.

POOLE, BARBER'S WHARF, TILES 2004 P72733

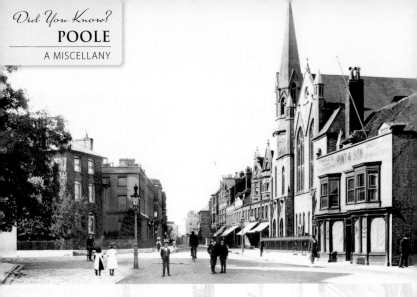

POOLE, HIGH STREET 1904 52808

In 1800 the town of Poole was still confined to the small peninsula
accessed either by sea or via a narrow neck of land at Town Gates
– where the Towngate Bridge arches over the railway line today.
Beyond the Town Gates was wild and largely uninhabited heathland,
with just a few farms at Longfleet and Parkstone. What little remains
of that heathland today is cherished, but a directory of 1798
described it as 'a barren, dreary heath which affords no pleasant view
to travellers who come from the more delightful part of the country'.
Nowadays the greater part of Poole's population lives in the suburbs
which have sprawled across that heathland towards Bournemouth
and Wimborne, but when the photographs on these two pages were
taken, in the early 20th century, the residents still mostly lived in the
Old Town and around the Quays, as they had for hundreds of years.
The photograph on this page was taken looking south down the
High Street from outside Beech Hurst (see page 26) which is off to
the left. The building with the spire is the Methodist Church in the
High Street, which opened in 1880.

Much of Poole's High Street is now pedestrianised, and is topped by the modern Dolphin Centre, but it was originally the main route leading up from the Quay and waterfront areas, along which in the past all manner of goods and wares were carried and transported to local shops, as well as on to what was the Town Gate and out of town. If you look above the modern shop fronts at ground level along the High Street you can still see some interesting indications of former times, such as various architectural details and decoration as well old trade advertising signs for business that are now long-gone.

The thatched cottage seen on the left of this photograph, on the corner of Carter Lane and High Street, survived until 1919. It was the home of the Town Crier and bill poster – a notice in the window reads 'Poole Bill Posting Company'. The cottage was replaced by Poole's first Woolworth's store. The prominent street clock on the right of this 1908 photograph can still be seen in the High Street; when this view was taken it graced the premises of watchmaker James Cole.

POOLE, HIGH STREET 1908 61164

The ironmonger's premises of W J Bacon in this photograph was on the corner of the Cornmarket and the High Street. It stood on the site of an old house called The Priory, and used to bear a plaque recording that King Charles II and his illegitimate son the Duke of Monmouth attended a banquet there on 15th September 1665. The shop was demolished in 1972 and replaced with Latimer House, and the plaque is now set into a wall nearby. At the time of King Charles's visit The Priory belonged to Colonel William Skutt, who had been the Parliamentarian captain of the local volunteers during the Civil War and called 'that arch-traitor' by the Royalists after his involvement in the first siege of nearby Corfe Castle in 1643, so hosting the king to dinner was a significant rapprochement. The Corporation Record Book of Poole recounts that King Charles visited Brownsea Island after having lunch at the house of local merchant Peter Hiley in the High Street, then returned to Poole Quay *'from whence he went on foot to the house of the said Colonel Skutt…the sheriff going before and the Mayor and Edward Man, Senior Bailiff bearing their maces before him',* and enjoyed *'a stately banquet…'.*

POOLE, HIGH STREET 1900 46088

POOLE, LONGFLEET ROAD 1904 52811

Falkland Square and the Dolphin Centre now occupy the land in the foreground of this view of Longfleet Road in 1904. The trams in this photograph were an efficient form of transport that had just been introduced to Poole, harnessing the power of the newly-introduced electricity – the power lines are seen above them in this view. The area's first tramline was launched in 1901, paving the way for a tram system that spanned the three boroughs of Poole, Bournemouth and Christchurch and by 1919 was carrying 20 million people a year. The trams remained an arterial public transport system until 1936.

Many of Poole's important industries of the past were related to its maritime location, such as boat and ship-building, and sail, net and rope-making. Poole used to have at least three rope walks, situated at Hamworthy, Baiter and on a site now occupied by the bus station at the Dolphin Centre, where women from the nearby rope factory 'walked' dressed strands of fibre into long lengths of rope – giving the area the name of Ladies Walking Field. This rope walk is commemorated nowadays in the name of Walking Field Lane, near Seldown Bridge.

POOLE, LUXURY SUNSEEKERS AT HAMWORTHY 2004 P72738

By the early 19th century there were five ship-building yards at
Hamworthy. Poole's own version of the 'Marie Celeste' mystery is the
story of the 'Mountaineer', a schooner built at Hamworthy in 1836
by William Cox and Thomas Slade senior. In 1850 the 87-ton vessel
failed to return from a voyage to Newfoundland and was given up
for lost. Then on 19th October that year she was found drifting 150
miles off the coast of Labrador, crewless but with her cargo of salt
intact. Strangely, not only was there no sign of life on board, but there
were no personal possessions either – apart from three miniature
portraits, found in the captain's locker, of Queen Victoria's daughter
Princess Alice. The 'Mountaineer' was brought home to Poole and
in June 1851 she was re-registered by Robert Slade of John Slade &
Company before resuming a career which continued for some years.
Of her crew who disappeared in 1850, however, nothing more was
heard. The boat-building tradition still continues in the town, which is
particularly famous for the luxury motor-yachts made by Sunseeker
International Ltd in its Poole shipyards.

When the railway first arrived in Dorset in 1847, Poole was not very well served, its only station being on the Hamworthy side of the water at the end of a branch off the London & Southern Western Railway's Southampton to Dorchester line. It was not until 1872 that Poole itself acquired a railway station, and the line was extended to the rapidly growing seaside resort of Bournemouth two years later. The swift development of Bournemouth had a great effect on Poole's economy. Poole was well placed to help provide materials needed for the new buildings, with roofing slates from North Wales arriving at Poole Quay as well as timber from North America and the Baltic. Prospering timber merchants J T Sydenham and J J Norton had their own wharves on the West Quay. The Asda store now stands on the site of Norton's yard, but Sydenhams is still in business. As well as the brisk trade in imported timber, coal and grain were also regularly arriving to fuel and feed the growing population. Several large mills appeared to handle the grain, including the Oakley brothers' granary in Paradise Street from the 1870s; Belben brothers' steam flour mill built on the Quay in 1864; and corn merchant W H Yeatman's Victoria steam-operated mill, also on the Quay, which was converted from a former warehouse in 1880 for use as a mill and continued in this role until 1974. To meet demand, and to accommodate ships of a deeper draught, the Quay was extended in 1893-95.

POOLE, SYDENHAMS TIMBER YARD, HAMSWORTHY 2004
P72718

Ships today tend to dock at Hamworthy, but within living memory the old Quay was busy with coal being unloaded into railway trucks which were pulled along the Quay by steam engines. The railway lines along Poole Quay ran for over half a mile along West Quay Road to join the main line at Sterte Road. They were laid in 1874 but became redundant in 1960 and soon disappeared. A gantry used for unloading coal from the ships into the trucks can be seen in the distant background of this view, beyond which was the pottery business that in the mid 20th century became the world-famous Poole Pottery. This business was founded in 1873 when Jesse Carter took over a failing ornamental brick and tile factory on the Quay. He originally established his business to make bricks and tiles, as 'Carter's Industrial Tile Manufactory', using the local ball clay found around Poole Harbour, and the millions of tiles that line the tunnels of the London Underground Railway were made and supplied by Carter's of Poole. Carter's distinctive green tiles can be seen on the façade of the Poole Arms pub on the Quay, perhaps the oldest building on the waterfront.

POOLE, BARGES AT THE QUAY
1908 61171

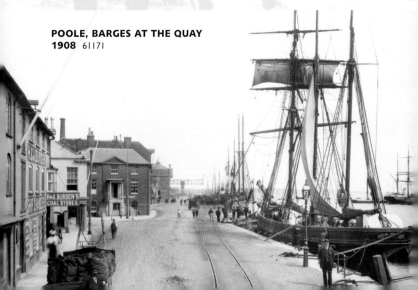

POOLE, THE QUAY 2004 P72741

Under the control of Jesse Carter's sons, Owen and Charles, and
following several name changes, the Carter's brick and tile business
became Poole Pottery, a leading name in the field of collectable
domestic and ornamental ware, famous for its simple, hand-painted
patterns. Poole Pottery maintained kilns on the end of the Quay
from 1873 until 2000, when production moved elsewhere in the
town. The site of the Poole Pottery premises on the Quay has
now been redeveloped into the Dolphin Quays complex of shops,
restaurants and luxury flats, as seen in the background of this
modern photograph. Poole Pottery has had a turbulent history in
recent years and is now owned by Lifestyle Group Ltd, part of Royal
Stafford Tableware Ltd. The main Poole Pottery factory is now in
Burslem in Stoke on Trent, but there is still a Poole Pottery shop and
working studio on the Quay, where visitors can watch modellers and
artists at work.

An old pub on the Quay is the Portsmouth Hoy, named after a type of ship that plied the coastal trade between Portsmouth and Poole and used to moor along this part of the Quay. Hoys were small vessels, usually rigged as sloops, which were used to carry passengers and cargo short distances along the coast and on the Thames. It was from these ships that came the nautical cry of 'Ahoy', used to hail a hoy to stop and take on a passenger.

A nice way to explore the town's heritage is to follow 'The Poole Cockle Trail', a walk around the Old Town that was opened in 1998 to celebrate the 750th anniversary of Poole's first Charter. The Poole Cockle Trail leaflet can be obtained at the Poole Welcome Centre on Poole Quay, or downloaded from the Poole Tourism website. (www. pooletourism.com and search for The Cockle Trail.) The walk begins outside the Lord Nelson pub on the Quay and follows a series of 78 numbered cockle signs set into the ground, with each number corresponding to a point on the trail.

There are a number of interesting modern public artworks along Poole Quay. Opposite the entrance to the High Street is a modern metal viewing platform and sculpture by Sir Anthony Caro called 'Sea Music'. Further along is an intriguing piece of artwork by Simon Watkinson, set into the pavement; it is called 'A Parallel Plotter', and represents a navigational tool. On the Quayfront near where ferries depart for Brownsea Island in Poole Harbour is a life-size bronze sculpture by Alison Avery of Lord Robert-Baden Powell (1857-1941), commemorating Poole's historic connection with the Boy Scout movement. In 1907 Lord Baden Powell held an experimental camp for boys on Brownsea Island which laid the foundations for the Boy Scout movement, which he initiated not long afterwards. He deliberately chose 20 boys from different backgrounds to see how they would mix, including three from Poole and seven from Bournemouth. Poole has another connection with Lord Baden-Powell, as St Peter's Church in Parkstone was where he married Olave Soames from nearby Lilliput on 31st October 1912. The wedding was kept secret to avoid press intrusion, due to Baden-Powell's fame as a hero of the Boer War.

BROWNSEA ISLAND, FROM SANDBANKS
c1881 B236501x

Brownsea Island is the largest of a number of islands in Poole Harbour. It was originally called Branksea Island, deriving from its Anglo-Saxon name of 'Brunoc's island', but this was changed to Brownsea in 1903 by the then owner, Charles Van Raalte, to avoid confusion with Branksome on the mainland. The first castle on the island was a Tudor blockhouse built by Henry VIII in 1547. The present castle (the large building on the left of this photograph) was largely the work of the Colonel Waugh in the 19th century, who also attempted to develop the island by opening clay pits and potteries in its wildest corners. From 1927 until 1961 the castle was the home of Mary Bonham Christie who lived there as a recluse, allowing nature to take over the island, which was closed to visitors. Following her death, Brownsea was passed to the care of the National Trust. It is now open to the public, although there is limited public access to the northern portion of the island, which is a Nature Reserve managed by Dorset Wildlife Trust and an important habitat for birds. The castle is not open to the public, as it is leased to the John Lewis Partnership as a holiday home for its employees, but the charming St Mary's Church on the island can be visited, part of which is dedicated to the Scouting movement.

SANDBANKS, POOLE HEAD 1904 52797

Unlike neighbouring Bournemouth, Poole did not become a holiday resort in any conventional sense until the mid 20th century, but remained important as a port and merchant centre. However, some of the sandier areas around Poole Harbour were attracting tourists by the late 19th and early 20th centuries such as the beach on Sandbanks, a small peninsula of land that guards the Poole side of Poole Harbour, reaching towards the opposite peninsula of Shell Bay and Studland. Now one of the most popular beaches in the area, this delightful view shows Sandbanks in its very early years as a seaside resort, looking east towards Poole Head, at the end of the long high cliff of Poole Bay that includes Canford Cliffs and Bournemouth, in the distance on the right. Sandbanks is now famously one of the most expensive places for property in Britain, but this photograph shows what it looked like in 1904, before the millionaires moved in!

The radio pioneer Guglielmo Marconi established one of the first radio stations in the world in 1898 at the Haven Hotel at Sandbanks, near the mouth of Poole Harbour. After setting up transmitting and receiving equipment and a 100ft mast there, he was able to receive radio signals which were transmitted from the small radio station he had established near The Needles on the Isle of Wight. The early experiments that he conducted for some time at Sandbanks led to him achieving a great milestone in communications history three years later, when he sent the first trans-Atlantic radio message from Poldhu Cove in Cornwall to St John's in Newfoundland. Marconi's radio masts can be seen in the background of this view of the Haven Hotel, taken in 1900. The small building in the foreground of this view was a coastguard lookout; the site where it stood is now the docking point for the chain ferry crossing the narrow strait of water between Sandbanks and the opposite peninsula of Shell Bay that forms the entrance to Poole Harbour.

SANDBANKS, THE HAVEN HOTEL 1900 46102

A major development for the town was the construction in 1834 of the first bridge between Poole town and Hamworthy, previously linked only by ferry. The wooden structure included a hand-operated swing section in the middle to allow ships to pass through. However, its steep gradient proved challenging for horse-drawn traffic, and in 1885 it was replaced by a flatter iron girder swing bridge with easier gradients, known as Hamworthy Bridge (photograph 52816). These first two bridges were both toll bridges. The first bridge that was free to cross was the third, Poole Bridge, a lifting bridge which replaced Hamworthy Bridge and opened in 1927 amid great celebrations (photograph 84910, opposite). Poole Bridge is still in use today, but a fourth bridge has now been constructed a little way alongside it – the spectacular Twin Sails lifting bridge, designed to resemble two sails of a yacht when the triangular twin bascules are raised, which opened to traffic in April 2012. The old and new bridges work in tandem, with the water between them used as a holding bay for boats. This allows at least one bridge to be available to road traffic for most of the time, thus improving traffic flow and reducing delays.

POOLE, HAMWORTHY BRIDGE 1904 52816

One of the most significant events for Poole in the 19th century was the purchase of Canford Manor and its estate in 1846 by Sir John and Lady Charlotte Guest. Sir John Guest was a Welsh engineer and entrepreneur who had made a vast fortune as the owner of the world's largest ironworks at Dowlais, South Wales. Between 1867 and 1904 the growing town of Poole and its surrounding area benefited from the philanthropy of their son Sir Ivor Guest and his wife, Lady Cornelia, the first Lord and Lady Wimborne. They built churches for fast-growing Broadstone and Upper and Lower Parkstone, initiated the building of schools at Broadstone and Longfleet, and also gave Broadstone and Parkstone their first golf courses.

Lady Wimborne was determined to give Poole a hospital, and began by opening a small infirmary for the poor in West Street in 1888, followed in 1890 by a larger 30-bed hospital in the Poole Mansion in Market Street. Finally, she persuaded her husband to provide the two-and-a-half acre site at Longfleet on which the new Cornelia Hospital opened in 1907. The Cornelia Hospital was renamed Poole General Hospital in 1948. Although the original buildings have been demolished, Lady Cornelia's hospital formed the beginning of the huge complex that is now the Poole Hospital NHS Foundation Trust.

POOLE, POOLE PARK 1904 52802

To mark Queen Victoria's Golden Jubilee in 1887, Lord and Lady Wimborne donated two large parcels of land to create parks for the town, Parkstone Park and Poole Park, an exceptionally generous gift. When Poole Park was completed, the Prince of Wales (the future King Edward VII) came to stay with Lord and Lady Wimborne at Canford Manor (now Canford School) in January 1890 before performing the opening ceremony. However, the severe overnight weather forced him to formally declare the park open while standing in Poole Station. Given to the town to be 'The People's Park', the popular recreational area of Poole Park now comprises 109.5 acres, of which 60 acres are water.

The huge salt-water lake in Poole Park is part of Poole Harbour's Parkstone Bay; it was enclosed on the south side when the Bournemouth to Poole railway line was built in 1874. Sluice gates in the railway embankment are used to maintain the water level and avoid tidal changes. However, another small, fresh-water, lake in Poole Park was created when the road on the right of photograph 61177 (below) was built across a corner of the park's large sea-water lake. Nowadays Poole Park's popular miniature narrow gauge railway runs for half a mile around this smaller lake and the road. The 10.25 inch narrow gauge railway, laid in 1949, is one of the longest established in England. Steam was replaced by diesel in 1970, but the four carriages are from the original train. Swans on the lakes have long been a feature of Poole Park, although the Canada geese that are also found there now were not introduced until 1957.

Poole Park is also the location of the town's war memorial, dedicated in 1927, which honours the members of the Armed Forces from Poole who died in the First and Second World Wars of the 20th century.

POOLE, THE PARK LAKE 1908 61177

Poole was not subjected to sustained bombing campaigns during the Second World War between 1939 and 1945 but did suffer from sporadic raids and 'leftover' bombs dropped by enemy aircraft returning from other targets. Poole's worst day of the war was 27 March 1941, when a fighter-bomber dropped part of its load on the Bourne Valley Gasworks, killing 34 people. During the war German bombers were lured off course by decoy fires being lit on Brownsea Island, designed to resemble burning buildings. On one night alone, May 21-22 1942, all but nine of 166 tons of explosives earmarked for Poole landed harmlessly on Brownsea and the surrounding waters of the harbour.

Poole's many contributions to the Second World War effort included the mass production of landing craft for use in the D-Day invasion of France of 6 June 1944, particularly by J Bolson & Son, who turned their modest yacht yard into a major cog in the national production line. Bolson's yard alone was turning out Landing Craft Assault at the astonishing rate of one a day, making them the biggest producers of LCAs in Britain. The Dorset Yacht Company also built landing craft, while other firms such as Newmans, Sydenhams and Burt & Vick carried out work on pre-fabricated Mulberry harbours for use in the D-Day landings.

Poole was very much part of the whole D-Day operation; a substantial area on the Lake shore at Hamworthy became HMS Turtle, a major training centre for the D-Day landings, and Poole was one of the most important departure points for troops making the crossing over the Channel as part of Operation Overlord. By the end of May 1944 there were troops everywhere, and the harbour filled up with warships. A plaque on the roadside wall of the old Custom House on Poole Quay commemorates the 300-plus boats that sailed from the Quays of Poole on the night of 5 June 1944. The majority of troops were American, destined to go ashore on the Normandy beaches codenamed Utah and Omaha. Those who sailed that night were the first of 22,000 soldiers and 3,500 craft that were to leave for Normandy from Poole alone over the next few weeks.

One of the most unlikely roles that Poole played during the Second World War, and for a few years afterwards, was that of Britain's main international airport; the ink on the declaration of war in September 1939 was barely dry when the first of Imperial Airways' Short flying boats touched down on the harbour. The later merger of Imperial Airways and British Airways created the British Overseas Airways Corporation (BOAC), and gave Poole a fleet of 32 luxurious flying boats, travelling to destinations all over the world and involved in numerous war-related missions. A number of premises around the Quay, High Street and Salterns Pier at Lilliput were requisitioned to provide all the functions associated with an international airport, including customs, immigration, a passenger lounge, medical and administration facilities and cargo stores. The flying boats remained in Poole until 1948, during which time test cricketers, rugby stars, politicians, film stars and eastern potentates all passed through the Poole terminal. A launch ferried the passengers to aircraft moored like yachts off Brownsea Island, each like a ship, its name boldly painted on the bow. Eighteen tons of aircraft then gently lumbered off the water, and, once airborne, cruised away at a leisurely speed of a mere 160mph.

Throughout the Second World War, the heather-clad Ham Common along the northern shoreline of Poole Harbour hid underground fuel tanks for the civilian and military flying boats of BOAC and RAF Hamworthy. The secret nearly exploded one night when Luftwaffe bombs set the common ablaze. After the war, this area became Rockley Sands Caravan Park, which developed as one of Poole's great leisure centres in the second half of the 20th century. Rockley Sands was one of Britain's earliest holiday camps, and also boasted one of England's first supermarkets to cater for its visitors. In the 1960s around 100,000 visitors a year were holidaying at Rockley Sands Caravan Park, which covered some 600 acres of harbourside, heathland and pine wood and catered for family groups who wanted outdoor holidays with plenty of activities. Water-skiing was just one of the many new sports offered to its guests – as seen in the photograph on page 47.

45

SPORTING POOLE

A wide range of water sports takes place in Poole Harbour – these include kiteboarding, wind-surfing, jet-skiing, water-skiing, yachting, power-boating, rowing, and canoeing. The harbour is the home of several sailing clubs, as well as the Royal Motor Yacht Club, founded in 1905. Poole hosts Poole Week each year, one of the largest dinghy sailing regattas in the country. Sailing also provided Poole with the most successful sportsman in its history, Rodney Pattison, who won gold medals in the Flying Dutchman class in the 1968 and 1972 Olympics and a silver at the 1976 Games.

Poole Swimming Club was founded in 1931. The Channel swimmers Sam Rockett, Samantha Druce and Marc Newman all did their early swimming in Poole. Sam Rockett was the first Briton home in the 1950 International Cross-Channel race; Samantha Druce became the youngest person to swim the Channel at the age of 12 in 1983; and Marc Newman swam the Channel five times and won the World Cup for open water swimming in 1986 and 1988. Dorset's first Olympic swimmer, Karen Legg, who won five medals at the 2002 Commonwealth Games, also began her career with the local club.

RLSS Poole Lifeguards organise the annual Brownsea Island Swim, a Wild Swimming event where competitors raise money for charity by swimming around the island, a distance of around 7.2km (4.5 miles). For those who prefer to race on land, Poole Park hosts the annual Poole Festival of Running.

Poole Town FC was established in 1890 with the merger of two local sides, Poole Rovers and Poole Hornets. The club's nickname is 'The Dolphins' after the dolphin on Poole Borough Council's coat of arms, and its mascot is 'Dylan the Dolphin'. The Dolphins currently (2012) play in the Southern Football League Division One South & West. In 2010-11 the Dolphins won the Wessex League Championship for the 3rd time in a row.

Poole is famous for its motorcycle speedway team, the 'Poole Pirates', which is one of the best supported sides in the country. Speedway was first established at Poole Stadium in 1948, and Poole has gone on to become one of the leading speedway teams in the country, winning numerous titles including the British League Division One championship in 1969 and 1994. The Pirates now race in the Elite League, the top tier of speedway racing, and have won the Championship a number of times. Poole Stadium also hosts major internationals, and the Speedway World Cup final took place there in August 2004. Two famous names in the Pirates' history, who both won the Speedway World Championship title while riding for Poole, are Mark Loram (2000) and Tony Rickardsson (2001 and 2002). Poole has also had great success in the Speedway World Under 21 Championship, with Ron Preston (1979), Jason Crump (1995), Lee Richardson (1999), Krzysztof Kasprzak (2005) and Darcy Ward (2010) all winning the title whilst riding for the Pirates.

Poole also has a successful cycle speedway team, whose track is at Baiter.

POOLE, WATER-SKIING AT ROCKLEY SANDS c1960 P72243

QUIZ QUESTIONS

Answers on page 52.

1. Whereabouts in Poole can you find the terracotta eagle seen in the photograph on the opposite page?

2. Brownsea Island in Poole Harbour is a sanctuary for which rare and much-loved British creature?

3. Parkstone girls are famously pretty – and that's official! How so?

4. Why was the Poole United Resistance Committee formed in 1947?

5. The Latin motto on the coat of arms of Poole Borough Council is 'Ad Morem Villae De Poole'. What does this mean?

6. Which king is the King Charles pub in Thames Street of the Old Town named after?

7. The headquarters of which important maritime charitable organisation are located in Poole?

8. Which popular crispbread is made in Poole?

9. Poole's Dolphin Centre is the largest indoor shopping centre in Dorset. It originally opened in 1969 under a different name – what was it?

10. What fate befell Alderman Horatio Hamilton outside Poole's Guildhall in 1866?

RECIPE

CREAM OF CRAB SOUP

Poole still has a fleet of working fishing boats, and the local catch can often be bought direct from the fishermen on the Quay in season, especially at weekends. Many of Poole's fishermen nowadays are crab and lobster potters. Crabs are available all year round and are delicious eaten fresh as a dressed crab or in a crab salad, but can also be used to make this delicious creamy soup. You will need one large freshly cooked crab in its shell (or two smaller crabs) to produce about the weight of prepared crab meat needed for this recipe. Otherwise, buy ready-prepared fresh or frozen cooked crab in a mixture of dark and light meat. If using frozen crab meat, thaw it thoroughly before use.

> 25g/1oz butter
> 1 medium onion, peeled and finely chopped
> 1 celery stick, finely chopped
> 1 garlic clove, crushed
> 1½ tablespoonfuls plain flour
> 225g/8oz prepared weight of cooked crab meat,
>   half dark and half light
> 1.2 litres/2 pints fish or chicken stock
> 150ml/ ¼ pint double cream
> 30ml/2 tablespoonfuls dry sherry
> Salt and freshly ground black pepper

Melt the butter in a large pan. Add the chopped onion, celery and garlic and cook over a medium heat for a few minutes, stirring frequently, until softened and transparent but not browned. Remove the pan from the heat and stir in the flour. Put the pan back on the heat and gradually add the stock, a little at a time and stirring continually. Bring the mixture to the boil, stirring constantly as it thickens, then reduce the heat, add the dark crab meat and simmer gently for about 30 minutes, stirring occasionally. Remove the pan from the heat and allow the soup to cool a little, then liquidize it in a blender or processor and return it to the cleaned out pan. Season to taste with salt and freshly ground black pepper. Chop the light crab meat into very small pieces and stir it into the soup, together with the sherry and the cream. Reheat the soup before serving, but do not allow it to boil.

RECIPE

ANGELS ON HORSEBACK

Poole has long been famous for its oyster beds. The 18th-century historian John Hutchina wrote that from these beds 'there are several sloops loaded every year, and carried to the creeks in the mouth of the Thames, where they are laid to fatten, to supply the London markets. And in the catching of which upwards of 40 sloops and boats are employed for two months every spring…The last day's catching is…thrown back into the channels within the harbour, where they fatten, and supply the town and country'. Oysters are still farmed in Poole Harbour by Othniel Oysters Ltd, which produces around 400 tons of high quality Pacific Oysters a year. Retail customers can buy their oysters online from Dorset Oysters Ltd, as well as locally caught clams, mussels, scallops and crabs – see www.dorsetoysters.com. This recipe for oysters was a popular snack in Victorian times and still makes a delicious snack or appetizer for modern tastes.

16 oysters, removed from their shells
Fresh lemon juice
8 rashers of streaky bacon with their rinds removed
8 small slices of bread
Butter
Paprika, or a dash of Tabasco sauce (optional)

Pre-heat the oven to 200°C/400°F/Gas Mark 6. Sprinkle each oyster with a little lemon juice. Lay the bacon rashers on a board, slide the back of a knife along each one to stretch it and then cut it in half crosswise. Wrap a piece of bacon around each oyster and secure with a wooden cocktail stick. Arrange the bacon-wrapped oysters on a baking sheet. Put the oysters and bacon into the pre-heated hot oven and cook for 8-10 minutes. Whilst the bacon and oysters are cooking, toast the bread. When the bacon is cooked through, spread each slice of hot toast with butter, and place a bacon-wrapped oyster on top of each piece. Sprinkle with a little paprika or a dash of Tabasco sauce, if used, before serving.

QUIZ ANSWERS

1. This is one of the terracotta eagles on the pillars at the entrance to Poole Park. It was made at the South Western Pottery Company at what is now the junction of Conifer Avenue and Pottery Road, Lower Parkstone, founded in 1856 by George Jennings.

2. Red squirrels. The species is this country's only native squirrel, but it has been all but wiped out across most of England and Wales since the introduction of the larger grey squirrel from North America in 1876. Brownsea Island is one of the last refuges of the species in mainland Britain. Around 200 red squirrels live there, and the National Trust, which owns and manages the island, is keen to maintain the colony.

3. Poole has a unique place in the history of beauty contests in that it has provided not just one but two holders of the Miss World title, the international beauty pageant. Ann Sidney was given a civic reception after becoming Miss World in 1964, then Sara-Jane Hutt became the UK's fifth Miss World in 1983 – and both girls came from Parkstone.

4. Relations between Poole and Bournemouth hit an all-time low in 1947, when the Victorian resort made an audacious proposal to 'absorb' Poole; the objectors dubbed it 'the Bournemouth Grab'. A Poole United Resistance Committee was formed to lead the opposition, which included the Communist Party of Poole, all the political clubs and the Poole Housewives' League. The following year the Boundary Commission not only sided with the objectors, but also proposed to promote Poole to county borough status. The Borough of Poole was made a unitary authority in 1997, gaining administrative independence from Dorset County Council, and remains quite definitely a separate place from Bournemouth.

5. The motto on the coat of arms of Poole Borough Council means 'According to the custom of the Town of Poole' and derives from the Great Charter granted to Poole by Queen Elizabeth in 1568 (see page 11).

6. The King Charles pub in Thames Street is named after King Charles X of France, who fled to England following the July Revolution of 1830. After disembarking at Hamworthy the king and his family were taken to Lulworth Castle on the Isle of Purbeck. Beside one of the fireplaces in the main bar of the Antelope Hotel in the lower High Street is a framed copy of a handwritten account about the arrival of the exiled King Charles X and his passage through Poole Customs on 22nd August 1830. The King Charles pub was originally the New Inn, but was renamed in the exiled king's honour.

7. Poole is the location of the headquarters of the Royal National Lifeboat Institution. Outside the RNLI headquarters on West Quay Road is a striking and dramatic memorial sculpture designed by Sam Holland, in the form of a figure in a boat saving someone from the water. Around the base of the memorial are steel, wave-like bands engraved with the names of 778 lifeboat crew who lost their lives whilst saving others.

8. Ryvita, which has been made at Old Wareham Road in Poole since just after the Second World War.

9. The first shopping centre at what is now the Dolphin Centre opened in 1969 as an Arndale Centre, one of a nationwide chain of the first 'American-style' undercover shopping malls to be built in the United Kingdom.

10. In 1866 Alderman Horatio Hamilton died after being shot several times outside the Guildhall as he was leaving a council meeting, over a dispute with a harbour pilot, John King, concerning ownership of a boat. A bullet hole from the incident can still be seen on the side wall near the north east corner of the Guildhall.

FRANCIS FRITH

PIONEER VICTORIAN PHOTOGRAPHER

Francis Frith, founder of the world-famous photographic archive, was a complex and multi-talented man. A devout Quaker and a highly successful Victorian businessman, he was philosophical by nature and pioneering in outlook. By 1855 he had already established a wholesale grocery business in Liverpool, and sold it for the astonishing sum of £200,000, which is the equivalent today of over £15,000,000. Now in his thirties, and captivated by the new science of photography, Frith set out on a series of pioneering journeys up the Nile and to the Near East.

INTRIGUE AND EXPLORATION

He was the first photographer to venture beyond the sixth cataract of the Nile. Africa was still the mysterious 'Dark Continent', and Stanley and Livingstone's historic meeting was a decade into the future. The conditions for picture taking confound belief. He laboured for hours in his wicker dark-room in the sweltering heat of the desert, while the volatile chemicals fizzed dangerously in their trays. Back in London he exhibited his photographs and was 'rapturously cheered' by members of the Royal Society. His reputation as a photographer was made overnight.

VENTURE OF A LIFE-TIME

By the 1870s the railways had threaded their way across the country, and Bank Holidays and half-day Saturdays had been made obligatory by Act of Parliament. All of a sudden the working man and his family were able to enjoy days out, take holidays, and see a little more of the world.

With typical business acumen, Francis Frith foresaw that these new tourists would enjoy having souvenirs to commemorate their days out. For the next thirty years he travelled the country by train and by pony and trap, producing fine photographs of seaside resorts and beauty spots that were keenly bought by millions of Victorians. These prints were painstakingly pasted into family albums and pored over during the dark nights of winter, rekindling precious memories of summer excursions. Frith's studio was soon supplying retail shops all over the country, and by 1890 F Frith & Co had become the greatest specialist photographic publishing company in the world, with over 2,000 sales outlets, and pioneered the picture postcard.

FRANCIS FRITH'S LEGACY

Francis Frith had died in 1898 at his villa in Cannes, his great project still growing. By 1970 the archive he created contained over a third of a million pictures showing 7,000 British towns and villages.

Frith's legacy to us today is of immense significance and value, for the magnificent archive of evocative photographs he created provides a unique record of change in the cities, towns and villages throughout Britain over a century and more. Frith and his fellow studio photographers revisited locations many times down the years to update their views, compiling for us an enthralling and colourful pageant of British life and character.

We are fortunate that Frith was dedicated to recording the minutiae of everyday life. For it is this sheer wealth of visual data, the painstaking chronicle of changes in dress, transport, street layouts, buildings, housing and landscape that captivates us so much today, offering us a powerful link with the past and with the lives of our ancestors.

Computers have now made it possible for Frith's many thousands of images to be accessed almost instantly. The archive offers every one of us an opportunity to examine the places where we and our families have lived and worked down the years. Its images, depicting our shared past, are now bringing pleasure and enlightenment to millions around the world a century and more after his death.

For further information visit: www.francisfrith.com

INTERIOR DECORATION

Frith's photographs can be seen framed and as giant wall murals in thousands of pubs, restaurants, hotels, banks, retail stores and other public buildings throughout Britain. These provide interesting and attractive décor, generating strong local interest and acting as a powerful reminder of gentler days in our increasingly busy and frenetic world.

FRITH PRODUCTS

All Frith photographs are available as prints and posters in a variety of different sizes and styles. In the UK we also offer a range of other gift and stationery products illustrated with Frith photographs, although many of these are not available for delivery outside the UK – see our web site for more information on the products available for delivery in your country.

THE INTERNET

Over 100,000 photographs of Britain can be viewed and purchased on the Frith web site. The web site also includes memories and reminiscences contributed by our customers, who have personal knowledge of localities and of the people and properties depicted in Frith photographs. If you wish to learn more about a specific town or village you may find these reminiscences fascinating to browse. Why not add your own comments if you think they would be of interest to others? See **www.francisfrith.com**

PLEASE HELP US BRING FRITH'S PHOTOGRAPHS TO LIFE

Our authors do their best to recount the history of the places they write about. They give insights into how particular towns and villages developed, they describe the architecture of streets and buildings, and they discuss the lives of famous people who lived there. But however knowledgeable our authors are, the story they tell is necessarily incomplete.

Frith's photographs are so much more than plain historical documents. They are living proofs of the flow of human life down the generations. They show real people at real moments in history; and each of those people is the son or daughter of someone, the brother or sister, aunt or uncle, grandfather or grandmother of someone else. All of them lived, worked and played in the streets depicted in Frith's photographs.

We would be grateful if you would give us your insights into the places shown in our photographs: the streets and buildings, the shops, businesses and industries. Post your memories of life in those streets on the Frith website: what it was like growing up there, who ran the local shop and what shopping was like years ago; if your workplace is shown tell us about your working day and what the building is used for now. Read other visitors' memories and reconnect with your shared local history and heritage. With your help more and more Frith photographs can be brought to life, and vital memories preserved for posterity, and for the benefit of historians in the future.

Wherever possible, we will try to include some of your comments in future editions of our books. Moreover, if you spot errors in dates, titles or other facts, please let us know, because our archive records are not always completely accurate—they rely on 140 years of human endeavour and hand-compiled records. You can email us using the contact form on the website.

Thank you!

For further information, trade, or author enquiries
please contact us at the address below:

**The Francis Frith Collection, Oakley Business Park,
Wylye Road, Dinton, Wiltshire SP3 5EU.**
Tel: +44 (0)1722 716 376 Fax: +44 (0)1722 716 881
e-mail: sales@francisfrith.co.uk **www.francisfrith.com**